SOCCER

SCORE WITH STEM!

By K. C. Kelley

Consultant: Tammy Englund, science educator

BEARPORT
PUBLISHING

Minneapolis, Minnesota

Credits

Cover and Title Page, © dslaven/Shutterstock; Background image, © Vera Larina/Shutterstock; 5, © feelgood/Shutterstock; 6, © George Green/Shutterstock; 7, © Charlie Reidel/AP Images; 8, © Pressmaster/Shutterstock; 9 main, FocusStocker/Shutterstock; 9 bottom, © katatonia82/Shutterstock; 10, © Paul Bradbury/iStock; 11, © Jari Hindstrom/Shutterstock; 12, Courtesy Catapult; 13, © Virginie LaFour/Belga/Newscom; 14–15 © Halfpoint Media/Shutterstock; 15, © Joe Petro/Icon Sportswire/Newscom; 16–17, © Stef22/Dreamstime; 17 top, © Marcin Kadziolka/Shutterstock; 17 bottom, © Annegret Hilse/dpa/Alamy Live News; 18–19, © Dignity 100/Shutterstock; 19, Daniel/Wikimedia; 20–21, © Benny Marty/Shutterstock; 22–23, © Dmitri Lovetski/AP Images; 24–25, © Randy Litzinger/Icon Sportswire/Newscom; 26, © Phil Noble/AP Images; 27, © Paolo Bona/Shutterstock; 29, © Aleksey Sagitov/Shutterstock.

Bearport Publishing Company
Minneapolis, Minnesota
President: Jen Jenson
Director of Product Development: Spencer Brinker
Senior Editor: Allison Juda
Associate Editor: Charly Haley
Designer: Colin O'Dea

Produced by Shoreline Publishing Group LLC
Santa Barbara, California
Designer: Patty Kelley
Editorial Director: James Buckley Jr.

Library of Congress Cataloging-in-Publication Data

Names: Kelley, K. C., author.
Title: Soccer : score with STEM! / by K.C. Kelley.
Other titles: Soccer (Sports STEM)
Description: Minneapolis, Minnesota : Bearport Publishing Company, 2022. | Series: Sports STEM | Includes bibliographical references and index.
Identifiers: LCCN 2021001056 (print) | LCCN 2021001057 (ebook) | ISBN 9781636911779 (library binding) | ISBN 9781636911847 (paperback) | ISBN 9781636911915 (ebook)
Subjects: LCSH: Soccer--Juvenile literature. | Sports sciences--Juvenile literature.
Classification: LCC GV943.25 .K453 2022 (print) | LCC GV943.25 (ebook) | DDC 796.334--dc23
LC record available at https://lccn.loc.gov/2021001056
LC ebook record available at https://lccn.loc.gov/2021001057

For more information, write to Bearport Publishing, 5357 Penn Avenue South, Minneapolis, MN 55419. Printed in the United States of America.

Contents

Soccer and STEM

The U.S. women's soccer team needs a goal. Megan Rapinoe kicks a long, high pass up the field. The ball flies toward Alex Morgan. Morgan reaches out her foot and **traps** the ball, **absorbing** its energy. Then, she smacks a shot with the inside of her foot. The ball spins as it flies through the air and curves into the net! Goal!

The team rushes toward one another to celebrate. It's another win for the amazing team of players—and for STEM.

SCIENCE: From flying through the air to bouncing on the field, a soccer ball moves according to the rules of physics.

TECHNOLOGY: Discover how wearable tech and digital recordings tell us more about the game.

ENGINEERING: Modern stadiums are designed to help fans enjoy games in new and exciting ways.

MATH: Information about teams and players is gathered as numbers called **stats**. A winning score is just the beginning!

Alex Morgan has used skill and STEM to score more than 100 goals for the U.S. women's national team.

Bend the Ball

The striker is ready to take a free kick. But if he has any chance of making the shot, he has to get around the other team's wall of defenders. How will the player get the ball past that wall? The answer is a combination of skill and science.

When the player kicks the ball, it curves around the wall of defenders toward the net.

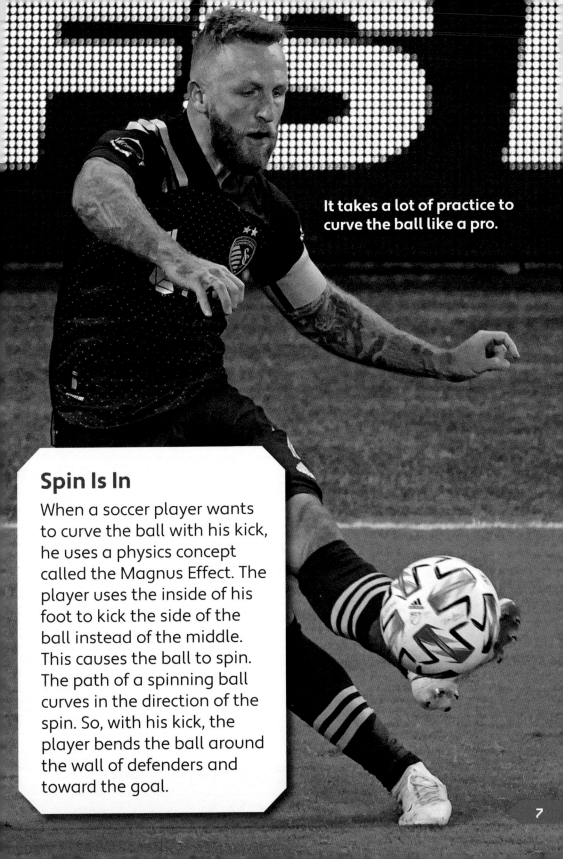

It takes a lot of practice to curve the ball like a pro.

Spin Is In

When a soccer player wants to curve the ball with his kick, he uses a physics concept called the Magnus Effect. The player uses the inside of his foot to kick the side of the ball instead of the middle. This causes the ball to spin. The path of a spinning ball curves in the direction of the spin. So, with his kick, the player bends the ball around the wall of defenders and toward the goal.

A Straight Shot

It's a breakaway! The forward streaks toward the goal. She sees an opening and kicks the ball, striking it with the laces of her shoe. The ball zooms in a straight line toward the corner of the goal. It flies into the back of the net. Goal!

Kicking directly behind a ball makes it go straight forward.

Pattern of Panels

Soccer balls can fly straight because of the design of the ball. The pattern of panels on a soccer ball helps keep air flowing smoothly over the whole ball. Ball designers used computer models and **wind tunnels** to find this pattern.

Black-and-white soccer balls were first used in the World Cup in 1970. That first black-and-white World Cup ball had 32 panels—12 black pentagons and 20 white hexagons. The pattern helped show players which way the ball was spinning. Today's pro balls may use even more colors.

The Key to Trapping

The midfielder kicks a pass, sending the ball through the air in a high arc. His teammate races to meet the ball. He extends his leg so that his foot touches the ball just as it comes down, then he immediately pulls his foot back slightly. *Bam!* The ball stops in front of him, and he is ready to make the next pass. It was a perfect trap!

The most basic trap is made by putting your foot on top of the ball.

Absorbing Energy

A soccer ball flying through the air has what's called **kinetic energy**, or energy of motion. To trap the ball, a soccer player has to absorb that energy. Players do this by pulling back wherever the ball hits them.

To make a chest trap, a player pulls back slightly to allow the ball to land lightly on his chest.

What are the ways a player can trap a soccer ball? She can use the bottom or side of her foot. She can also use her thighs, chest, or head. No matter which part of the body is used, every trap has to do the same thing—absorb the energy of a moving ball.

Gathering Game Data

After a long, hard game, players gather around the coach. They study charts and graphs on a computer. All of the information on the device came from the players themselves—during the game. **Sensors** in players' uniforms provide important **data** that can help win games.

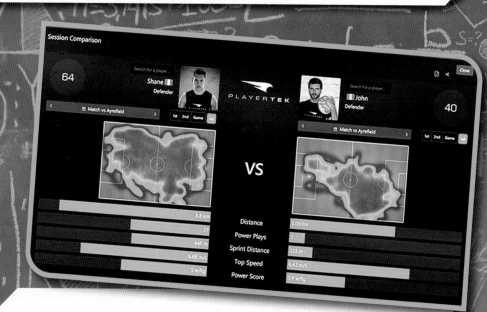

Gearing Up

Sensors in clothing that send information wirelessly to a computer are a kind of wearable tech. They can track how fast players run, where they move on the field, and how hard they kick. Players can improve by learning about their own speed and movement. Coaches use data from the sensors to show their teams how to play better together.

Sensors go in a pocket under a player's shirt.

Sensors are also built into some soccer balls. These sensors send information to an app that shows the direction, speed, and spin of the ball each time it's kicked.

DribbleUp®
APP ENABLED BALL
SIZE 5

Shoe Tech

Shoes are a soccer player's most important type of gear. For years, designers have been working to make soccer shoes better. They have tried many different shoe shapes and materials. Today's high-tech shoes are lightweight, flexible, and designed to help a player score the winning goal. How?

Soccer players need sturdy shoes with cleats that grip the ground.

Printed Shoes and Side Laces

Shoe companies use many materials to make soccer shoes. Most use leather, but some high-tech shoes are built with human-made fabrics. These materials are strong but lightweight. One company even uses a 3D printer to make custom-fit shoes out of thin, light plastics. Shoe laces are also getting a design upgrade. Instead of having laces on the top, some high-tech shoes have them on the side. This creates a flatter surface for kicking the ball with the top of the foot.

Carson Pickett

How do you tie a shoe if you have only one hand? International soccer star Carson Pickett has faced that question since she was a kid. She was thrilled to help Nike design a soccer shoe with no laces. A Velcro strap lets Pickett easily adjust her shoes with one hand.

Make the Right Call

The forward races toward the goal. He traps the ball, dribbles it once, and then an opponent slides in. The ball flies away, and the forward ends up on the ground. Foul! Or is it? The referee listens on her earpiece, then blows her whistle and draws a box in the air. It's time to check in with the video assistant referee (VAR)!

VAR in Action

In many pro leagues, an official carefully watches video as it records the game. If the official sees a play that the referee may have missed, the video-watcher radios the official on the field. Then, the referee can look at the video to see whether the right call was made. If the referee sees something on video that she did not see before, she can change the call.

Soccer is a fast-moving game, and it's difficult to see every play. To help, some referees wear goal watches. Cameras instantly record goals and send a signal that vibrates the watch. This alerts the referee and helps make sure that every goal is counted.

Two Fields in One

Fans have just finished cheering for the English soccer team Tottenham Hotspur. The beloved Spurs won another big game in the team's new stadium. But when the soccer game is over, stadium workers have a lot to do. Very soon, an American football game will be played in the same stadium by two National Football League (NFL) teams visiting from the United States. It's time to switch the pitch!

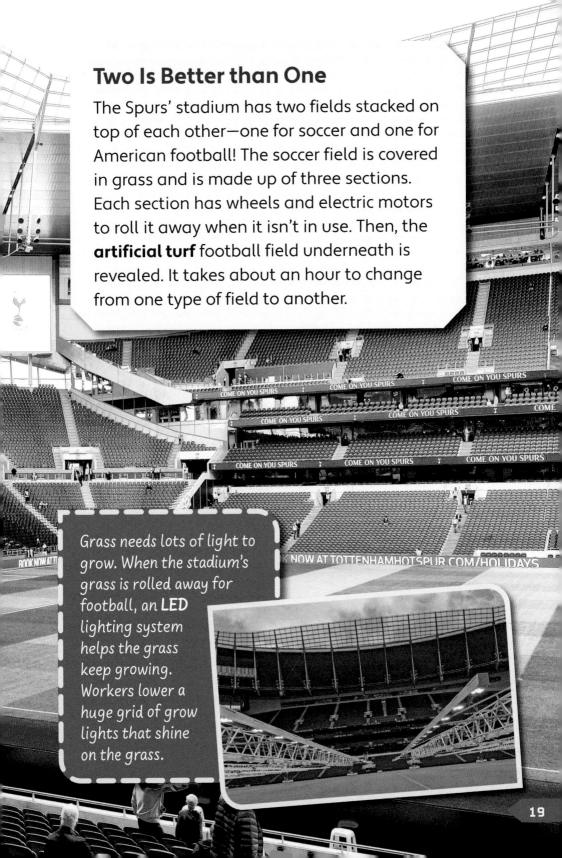

Two Is Better than One

The Spurs' stadium has two fields stacked on top of each other—one for soccer and one for American football! The soccer field is covered in grass and is made up of three sections. Each section has wheels and electric motors to roll it away when it isn't in use. Then, the **artificial turf** football field underneath is revealed. It takes about an hour to change from one type of field to another.

Grass needs lots of light to grow. When the stadium's grass is rolled away for football, an **LED** lighting system helps the grass keep growing. Workers lower a huge grid of grow lights that shine on the grass.

19

World Cup Stadiums

In 2010, FIFA, the international organization for soccer, announced the host country for the 2022 World Cup tournament. Soccer fans around the world were surprised by the pick—Qatar, a small country with very hot temperatures. The heat could be uncomfortable or even dangerous for fans and players! But Qatar was prepared to solve this problem.

One of seven stadiums built in Qatar

A Cool Building Boom

Qatar built seven new stadiums for the 2022 World Cup. To keep cool in the extremely hot weather, engineers found a way to put air conditioning in outdoor stadiums. Cold water is pumped beneath the stadiums. This water is used to create cool air, which is then pushed out of vents located under each of the stadium's seats. Large fans also blow the cool air to the field, keeping the players comfortable and safe during games.

Keeping Possession

Late in the game, the home team holds the lead and controls the ball. The players make pass after pass. They need to keep **possession** of the ball so their opponents do not score. Finally, time runs out—the home team wins!

Controlling the Ball

A key soccer stat is possession **percentage**. This is a measure of which team controls the ball most during a game. Possession changes when a team **intercepts** a pass or the ball goes out of bounds. Often, a team has a better chance of winning if they keep control of the ball for longer.

To figure out possession percentage, take the total amount of possession time for a team and divide by the total game time. Then, move the decimal point two spots to the right.

Passing the ball can help a team keep possession.

Goalies Need Geometry

The striker dribbles down the side of the field toward the opponent's goal. As she nears the net, the goalie rushes out to meet her. The striker tries to kick the ball past the goalie, but the goalie swats it away, using quick hands—and geometry!

The goalie in yellow races out to make a big stop.

Cut the Angle

A goalie's job is to stop the ball from going over the goal line and into the net. But they rarely stand on the goal line. By moving out and away from the goal, goalies cut down the possible **angles** for shooters. This means they reduce the amount of space where opponents can score. Moving away from the goal line lets goalies better protect their goals.

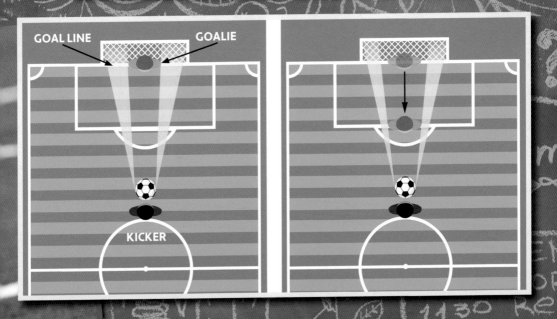

GOAL LINE   GOALIE

KICKER

The goalpost closest to the player shooting the ball is called the near post. By blocking the path to the near post, a goalie makes a shooter aim toward the far post. That's a much longer and harder shot to make!

Who's Number One?

Liverpool, a team in the English Premier League (EPL), had not won the league championship for 30 years. Finally, in July 2020, Liverpool earned enough points to win the EPL! The team won 32 games, tied 3, and lost 3. That gave them 99 points—the highest in the EPL that season!

It is relatively common for soccer games to stay tied for most or all of a game.

Win, Lose, or Draw

In most soccer leagues, including the EPL, teams earn three points in league standings for each win. They earn one point for a tie score and no points for a loss. Teams are ranked in their leagues not by who wins the most games, but by who earns the most points. A team could win the most games but not win the league championship. How? The league winner might have scored more points in ties than a team with more wins.

Lifting the English Premier League trophy is a great honor for the winning team.

Do the Math!

It's time to do some soccer math! Learn how to calculate three types of stats. Then, do the math to find out which players had the best stats.

Adding Goals

Players can score goals for club or country. Add the number of each kind of goal to see the total goals scored.

1. Which player scored the most goals?

PLAYER	CLUB GOALS	COUNTRY GOALS
Cristiano Ronaldo	646	102
Lionel Messi	640	71

Save Percentages

A percentage is a part of a whole number expressed in hundredths. And a save percentage is a stat that shows how often a goal was stopped. To find the percentage, divide the number of saves each goalie made by the number of shots they faced, and then move the decimal point two units to the right.

2. Which goalie had a better save percentage?

PLAYER	SAVES	SHOTS FACED
Alyssa Naeher	64	82
Aubrey Bledsoe	54	66

3. **Which goalie had a better percentage of saving penalty shots?**

PLAYER	SAVES	PENALTY SHOTS FACED
Gianluigi Buffon	79	307
Manuel Neuer	94	341

Per-Game Averages

A per-game average is a number that helps show how well a player did in more than one game. To find it, divide the total number of goals by the number of games played.

4. **Which player had the higher goals-per-game average?**

PLAYER	GOALS	GAMES
Alex Morgan	107	169
Abby Wambach	185	244

Answers:
1. Ronaldo has more goals. He scored 748 to Messi's 711.
2. Bledsoe's percentage of 81.8 was better than Naeher's 78.0, even though Naeher made more saves.
3. Neuer's save percentage of 27.6 is better than Buffon's 25.7.
4. Morgan scored an average of 0.63 goals per game, but Wambach's 0.76 was better.

Glossary

absorbing taking another force or object into one's self

angles spaces between intersecting lines

artificial turf a human-made playing surface that looks like grass

data information often in the form of numbers

intercepts prevents something from reaching the intended destination

kinetic energy energy that is in motion

LED stands for light emitting diode; an energy-efficient way of producing light

percentage a part of a whole, expressed as a number out of one hundred

possession ownership or control

sensors electronic devices that gather and record information

stats short for statistics; information stated as numbers

traps brings a moving soccer ball to a stop and under one's control

wind tunnels enclosed spaces where fast-moving air is blown against objects to learn about air flow

Read More

Havelka, Jacqueline. *STEM in Soccer (Connecting STEM and Sports).* Broomall, PA: Mason Crest, 2019.

Marquardt, Meg. *STEM in Soccer (STEM in Sports).* Minneapolis: Abdo Publishing, 2018.

McCollum, Sean. *Full STEAM Soccer: Science, Technology, Engineering, Arts, and Mathematics of the Game (Full STEAM Sports).* North Mankato, MN: Capstone Press, 2019.

Learn More Online

1. Go to **www.factsurfer.com**

2. Enter "**STEM Soccer**" into the search box.

3. Click on the cover of this book to see a list of websites.

Index

About the Author

K. C. Kelley has written more than 100 books on sports for young readers, including titles on basketball, soccer, baseball, the Olympics, and much more. He has worked for both *Sports Illustrated* and the National Football League.